Pebble® Plus

Physical Science

STATES OF MATTER

by Abbie Dunne

raintree

a Capstone company — publishers for children

Raintree is an imprint of Capstone Global Library Limited, a company incorporated in England and Wales having its registered office at 264 Banbury Road, Oxford, OX2 7DY – Registered company number: 6695582

www.raintree.co.uk
myorders@raintree.co.uk

Edited by Linda Staniford
Designed by Veronica Scott
Picture research by Eric Gohl
Production by Katy LaVigne

ISBN 978 1 474 72249 0
20 19 18 17 16
10 9 8 7 6 5 4 3 2 1

British Library Cataloguing in Publication Data
A full catalogue record for this book is available from the British Library.

Acknowledgements
We would like to thank the following for permission to reproduce photographs: Capstone Studio: Karon Dubke, 13; Shutterstock: Africa Studio, 17, Andrey Armyagov, 20 (bottom), Ilike, 11, Lori Sparkia, 19, mavo, cover, Pigprox, 15, studiots, 5, Tnymand, 9, vitalez, 7, Yevhen Tarnavskyi, 20 (top) Design Elements: Shutterstock

Every effort has been made to contact copyright holders of material reproduced in this book. Any omissions will be rectified in subsequent printings if notice is given to the publisher.

Printed and bound in China.

Contents

What is matter?

Everything in the world

is matter. Matter is anything

that takes up space.

Your bed and books are matter.

You are made of matter.

States of matter

Matter can be a solid, liquid or gas. Trees, rocks and buildings are solid. Rivers and lakes are liquid. The air is a gas.

Solids

Solids keep their shape and size.

Some solids are hard.

They don't bend easily.

Rocks, ice cubes and metal

are hard solids.

ice cubes
are solid

Some solids change shape easily.

You can form modelling clay
into different shapes.

Rope can be twisted into a knot.

Tree branches can bend.

Liquids

Liquids do not have their own shape. A liquid takes the shape of the container that holds it. Milk, water and shampoo are liquids.

Gases

Gases have no shape. They spread to fill the space they are in. Air is made of gases. You can feel air move on windy days.

Mixing solids and liquids

Some solids and liquids can be mixed together. Paint changes the colour of water. Salt dissolves in water. You can tell it is there if you drink the water.

Changing matter

Matter can change forms. Ice cream melts on a hot day. Water turns to ice in the freezing cold. Boiling water turns to steam.

Activity

Predict how a solid might change when it is put into water. Then do the following experiment to find out.

What you need

- permanent marker
- 2 sandwich-size self-sealing bags
- water
- ice cube
- antacid tablet
- camera or crayons and paper

What you do

1. Write "ice cube" on one bag. Write "antacid tablet" on the other bag.

2. Fill each bag half full of water.

3. Zip each bag almost closed until there is just enough room to squeeze in an ice cube or the antacid tablet.

4. Put the ice cube in the bag marked "ice cube". Squeeze the rest of the air out of it and zip it closed.

5. Put the antacid tablet in the bag marked "antacid tablet". Squeeze the rest of the air out of it and zip it closed.

6. Use the camera to record what you see, or make a drawing of what happened.

What do you think?

Make a claim. A claim is something you believe to be true.

How do some solids change when placed in water?
Use the results of your experiment to support your claim.

Glossary

dissolve   disappear into something else

gas   something that is not solid or liquid and does not have a definite shape

liquid   matter that is wet and can be poured, such as water

matter   anything that has weight and takes up space

solid   substance that holds its shape

Find out more
Books

Experiments in Material and Matter with Toys and Everyday Stuff (Fun Science), Natalie Rompella (Raintree, 2015)

Matter and Materials (Hands-on Science), Peter Mellett (Kingfisher Books, 2013)

What Is It Made Of? Noticing Types of Materials, Martha E. H. Rustad (Millbrook Press, 2015)

Websites

www.bbc.co.uk/bitesize/ks2/science/materials/solids_liquids_gases/read/1/

This site has information about states of matter.

resources.woodlands-junior.kent.sch.uk/revision/science/changingmaterials.htm

This site has interactive games and activities about materials and states of matter.

www.bbc.co.uk/bitesize/ks2/science/materials/gases_liquids_solids/play/

This site has an interactive game about the differences between solids, liquids and gases.

Comprehension questions

1. When water freezes, which state of matter does it become?

2. Explain some features of matter that is liquid.

3. Liquids take the shape of the container they are in. What do you think happens when a liquid is spilled?

Index